INTO IT

INTO IT

LAWRENCE JOSEPH

FARRAR,

STRAUS

AND

GIROUX

NEW YORK

FARRAR, STRAUS AND GIROUX
19 Union Square West, New York 10003

Copyright © 2005 by Lawrence Joseph
All rights reserved
Distributed in Canada by Douglas & McIntyre Ltd.
Printed in the United States of America
First edition, 2005

Grateful acknowledgment is made to the editors of *After Ovid: New
Metamorphoses, Commonweal, Jacket, The Kenyon Review, The KGB
Bar Book of Poems, The London Review of Books, Michigan Quarterly
Review, Ontario Review, Pequod, Poetry, Subtropics,* and *TriQuarterly,*
where poems in this book first appeared, some in earlier versions.
"Unyieldingly Present" appeared in *Siècle 21* in French translation
by Catherine Pierre-Bon. The quotation in the invocation is from
Ovid: The Metamorphoses, translated and edited by Horace Gregory
(Viking Press, 1958). The quotation in the epigraph is from *Letters
of Wallace Stevens* (Alfred A. Knopf, 1966).

Library of Congress Control Number: 2005928915
ISBN-13: 978-0-374-17569-6
ISBN-10: 0-374-17569-1

Designed by Gretchen Achilles

www.fsgbooks.com

10   9   8   7   6   5   4   3   2   1

. . . give me the voice
To tell the shifting story . . .
—OVID, *The Metamorphoses*

Moreover, in the world of actuality . . . one is always living a little out of it. There is a precious sentence in Henry James, for example, for whom everyday life was not much more than the business of living, but, all the same, he separated himself from it. The sentence is . . . "To live in the world of creation—to get into it and stay in it—to frequent it and haunt it—to think intensely and fruitfully—to woo combinations and inspirations into being by a depth and continuity of attention and meditation—this is the only thing."

—WALLACE STEVENS

CONTENTS

INTO IT

IN IT, INTO IT, INSIDE IT, DOWN IN

How far to go?—I have to, I know,
I promised. But how? How, and when?

And where? It was cold. The sky,
blue, almost burst, leaves burnished

yellow. Nearing Liberty, Liberty
and Church streets. So it happened

in early November. Which is to say
a story took place. Once again

new lines, new colors. One scene
and then another. Characters talking

to one another. It was she who
opened the conversation. "A wild rose,

and grapes on vines along the ground,
a butterfly on the green palmetto,

plums the size of walnuts, gray
and vermilion"—she sat up straighter,

lips pressed together, looking me
square in the eyes—"and why, you tell me why,

in this time of so many claims to morality,
the weight of violence

is unparalleled in the history
of the species . . ." What needs to be said—

why not say it? "Who dares to learn
what concerns him intimately,"

is how he says it in his book. Then the mind
runs through the spaces left behind, crossing

over to a different place. It certainly was
a well-dressed crowd. Here, again, the General,

the Attorney General, a beeper in one hand,
a crucifix in the other; here, again,

language, a language—a style, a groove, a fate.
On the esplanade, Battery Park, a newspaper,

old, caught in a gust, a child,
lost, crying—the pain was ours, I know it now;

beauty, the answer, if you must know—
the sun ablaze on the harbor. Hearing

a sentence phrased in . . . a tenor? countertenor? . . .
an error of nature, after all—made

of thought and of sound, of feelings seen—
in it, into it, inside it, down in.

WHEN ONE IS FEELING ONE'S WAY

I

The sky was red and the earth got hot,
like a hundred degrees hot, I mean.
"Stay cool," the monk was said to have said,
"you've still got a long way to go."
A monk, say, of Hue, who, to protest
the killing of innocents, is dragging
an altar on—yes it was, Hillside Avenue.
So what else is new? One new
voice mail message. A woman,
a certain woman, has been seen, eyes,
liquid blue eyes, glistening with tears.

II

Two things, the two things that are interesting
are history and grammar.
In among the foundations of the intelligence
the chemistries of words. "The fault lines
of risk concealed in a monetary landscape . . ."
What of it? Nothing but the same resistance
since the time of the Gracchi—
against the arrogation by private interests
of the common wealth,
against the precious and the turgid language
of pseudoerudition (thugs,
thugs are what they are,

false-voiced God-talkers and power freaks
who think not at all about what they bring down).

III

A pause. Any evening, every evening.
When one is feeling one's way
the pattern is small and complex.
At center a moral issue, but composed,
and first. Looks to me like,
across the train yards, a blurred sun
setting behind the high ground
on the other side of the Hudson,
overhead purple and pink.
A changing set of marginal options.
Whole lots of amplified light.

IV

Oh, I get the idea. That image,
the focal point
of a concave mirror, is old.

And that which is unintermitted
and fragile, wild and fragile (there,
behind the freighter's yellow
puffs of smoke; God, no, I haven't

forgotten it) is, I said,
still fragile, still proud.

THE BRONZE-GREEN GOLD-GREEN FOREGROUND

The bronze-green gold-green foreground:
what can only be said in that language,

opaque, though clear, painted language.
The shy and green one, the most beautiful

one, the intensest one, on my mind,
opening, opened, in me . . . The reflection

(and, or, the refraction) of a reflection:
in light of that, light in secret . . .

(Tableaux: "Ancient Back Streets One November
Late Friday Afternoon" . . . "The Eyes the Sky's Blue" . . .)

Those places where the narratives began . . . there,
too, in the rain. The code changed again.

I NOTE IN A NOTEBOOK

Pink sunlight, blue sky, snowed-upon January morning.
The romantic restated—a woman and a man
by themselves, each alone in the other. Those
transcriptions of the inexpressible—perhaps
the experience of having heaven
is just simply perfect luck . . . That winter,
on Belle Isle, the ice floes, the Seven Sister
smokestacks. In Angel Park, a figure in motion,
muted reds and grays, clouds and light, and shadows
in motion, a freezing wind out of Canada
over the lake. A figure, in the factory
behind the Jefferson Avenue Assembly, marking
and filing the parts of the new model prototype
Chryslers, standing at a window, smoking a Kool.
Those with the masks of hyenas are the bosses,
and those wearing mass-produced shirts and pants,
among them my father . . . Cavafy's poem, the one
about how if he's wasted his life in this corner
of the world he's wasted it everywhere. What
is happening, what is done. Convicted
of rape and murder, he leaves a piece of pie
in his cell, believing he'll be able to eat it
after he's electrocuted—the fact that a compound,
1, 3-diphenyl propane, forged from the fires'
heat and pressure, combined with the Towers'
collapse, has never been seen before.
The technology to abolish truth is now available—
not everyone can afford it, but it is available—

when the cost comes down, as it will, then what?
Pasolini's desire to make, to write, an intricate,
yet rational mosaic, byzantine and worth, at least,
a second, or even a third, reading . . . An epical
turn, so great a turn—her voice in him,
his voice in her—the vista, a city,
the city, taking a shape and burning . . .

INCLINED TO SPEAK

I saw that. One woman, her personality
and appearance described as lovely,
while performing her predawn prayers,
watched the attackers shoot to death her husband,
her seven-year-old son, three of her brothers,
as they grabbed her four-year-old son from her arms
and cut his throat, taking her and her two sisters
away on horses and raping them. Of course it's genocide.
And, yes, it brings to mind I am constantly aware of,
in making the poem, Brecht's point, to write about trees—
implicitly, too, to write about pleasure—
in times of killing like these is a crime;
and Paul Celan's response, that for Brecht a leaf
is a leaf without a tree, that what kinds of times
are these when a conversation—Celan believed a poem
is a conversation—what kinds of times are these
when a poem is a crime because it includes
what must be made explicit.

                            What is seen, heard, and imagined
at the same time—that truth. A sort of relationship
is established between our attention
to what is furthest from us
and what deepest in us. The immense enlargement
of our perspectives is confronted
by a reduction in our powers of action, which reduces
a voice to an inner voice inclined to speak only
to those closest to us . . .

THE PATTERN-PARALLEL MAP OR GRAPH

The sky?—ultramarine, tinted black, lines
of black ink. Newspapers, mud, fishtails,
betel nuts, trampled on along Canal Street.

Luck turns out hot. Eros is extraordinarily
lucky to have found Psyche. According
to the story, which is taken from Apuleius,
Eros's and Psyche's bodies are wet and hot.

Nine years—where does that take us
on the pattern-parallel map or graph?
Nine years from two thousand—nineteen ninety-one . . .
Wallace Stevens—him again—
in his commonplace book,
an entry made in nineteen thirty-four:
"Ananke is necessity or fate personified,
the saeva Necessitas of Horace
Odes Book I No. 35, to Fortune . . ."

I'm the one who hears it. Chromatically
suspended, as the notes feel their way
from intervals to motifs, a progression
in a manner that disguises the key—
a linear polyphony forming harmonies in strange
developments. All kinds of different stuff, mixed
and fused, is where it's at, chunks of vibrato . . .
Simultaneity requires the use of a topological
logic. Time compressed—interactivity escalated

to maximum speed. Why not? Have their official
status changed from human to animal, they live like
animals already. Once they've attained animal status
dozens of groups will come forward to defend them.
What, let's say, in twelve years
will the zone of suffering that exists
outside the established orders look like? There's
Venus again, moving across the sun,
in a mini-eclipse visible twice every century or so.
There's the achieved conception, a God
accessible and inaccessible, merciful
and just, human and divine, completed
not far from the Black Sea. That mood,
intensely subjective, scenes and myths
reemerged. There, on the table, a flower the yellow
of flax closes, the irises unfolding,
two of them deep blue-purple, a third is larger,
and china blue. There, small, bright birds
in wooden cages in a store on East Broadway,
an illuminated scroll unrolled on the counter.

WOODWARD AVENUE

The destination, the destiny, a street,
an avenue. When General MacArthur, deviating
from his itinerary, was driven out
to the Shrine at Twelve Mile Road
and Woodward to help in Coughlin's
rehabilitation. History followed
in the direction of a more or a less
cosmological evolution. On the ground
the authorities began to sense the situation
was going to get worse before it got better.
Around midnight the street was blocked,
a man, backed up against a white
Mustang, was beaten. What was it like?
The essential principles were power,
accuracy, economy, system, and speed.
The Highland Park plant was known
as the Crystal Palace because of its expanse
of windows. Moving assembly lines, conveyor
belts, gravity feeds, and railroads
constituted the materials-handling
network, portrayed, metaphorically, as a wave
of production. No singularities.
In Paperbacks Unlimited, an essay,
"The Law of Love and the Law of Violence,"
in a book of pamphlets and essays by Tolstoy.
The struggle for the "imperium mundi" down to
a not so sudden sorrow. My father
listens to the radio, reading. The past

rearranged by hardening arteries.
My grandfather's voice doesn't leave me.
So many voices, which of them to be taken
seriously? Am I mistaken or was napalm
transported by teamsters from Midland?
Am I not correct in saying that for purposes
of insurance there was considerable dispute
as to whether it was a war, a riot,
or an insurrection? An arm's snapped,
a body's kicked down darkened stairs,
a face is spit into, one of the babies
is left to die. The Greek dictionary
lies on the kitchen table. There's a torn
photograph of the Blessed Sacrament
grade school basketball team, and, here,
a ticket stub from the championship game
held in the Memorial Building. Screaming
all day about war. Screaming that nothing
can be solved. Only the very poorest spirits
can't be roused by the practical, where we
literally are, approach. Remember that?
The heavyweight champion of the world, found
in a stupor without his false teeth, naked
in the backseat of his Continental convertible
in the parking lot of The Last Chance Bar.
Neither the proclamation nor the plea
had any effect. The men of the 701st
Military Police Battalion in full battle gear,

bayonets fixed at high port, moving through
Cadillac Square to disperse the mob of over
ten thousand. He was, Henry Ford said,
not in the business of making cars
but in the business of making money.
The Algiers Motel? U-shaped, with neon lights,
swimming pool lined by a metal fence
and faded beach umbrellas, the style
Florida Gulf Port traditional, set
back from the street, a rusted Carte Blanche
sign swinging on a post out front.
Reality explained. Those corners where
the little one curled up and went to sleep
when she was tired, where, when she was
unsure of herself, she secretly went to cry.
I can smell something cooking—I can tell
there's going to be a feast. A thickish
film sticks to the windshields and the lungs,
dawn is burnt red along the landscape's rim.
Smoke that sketches the sky with gray.
Gray. Smoke-gray. The mist lifts.
So drive this street and drop into
this hell where a man was once cut
from ear to ear. High winds again,
an unexpected chill. A soft, misty, rain.
Patches of pavement oiled and streaked
with rain. The appointed time, in detail—
the crazy weave of the perfect mind.

How much later, the light snow lay encrusted
on the oak leaves until the wind turned
a leaf over. The wind blowing constantly.
Can you get to it? A dance that you get to,
"The Double-Clutch." Listen. Sure is funky.
Everyone clapping their hands, popping
their fingers, everyone hip, has walks.
Effects are supplied, both rhythmic
and textual. Another take? Same key?
Sometimes you've just got to improvise a bit
before you're in a groove. Listen.
That's right. It's an illumination.
That which occurs in authentic light.
Like the man said. So many selves—
the one who detects the sound of a voice,
that voice—the voice that compounds
his voice—that self obedient to that fate,
increased, enlarged, transparent, changing.

ON THAT SIDE

April and May. There, very near,
dimensions imploded—
the point, the line, the surface.
The arrangement of power, the immanence
of the pressure. "What,"
he said with a laugh, "you think I'm exaggerating?"

I can't say that I've internalized it all yet.
I'm over on the other side—
Green Dolphin Street, the bar and café, that is,
a table in back, in the garden, engaged
in an act of asceticism.
A memory—so vivid, I close my eyes.

WHAT DO YOU MEAN, WHAT?

It's foreground—or is it background?—
this individual and collectivized looting
of the most astonishing complexity,
each point of an imagined circuit
attached to each of the others . . .

In the King James Hotel in a bath towel,
solicitous with the interviewer
who crosses her long, tanned legs, smiling at him
when he says you need a billion
just to get into the game; on my way downtown
(no, he answers, he doesn't own his own taxi),
his name is Thomas Saint Thomas, a green card
is what he owns, a working man from Haiti—
he'll play for me (I, perhaps, have not yet heard)
a tape cassette of a speech
concerning the imminent coming of Jesus Christ
Word Incarnate, Second Person of the Triune God,
who'll whip the moneylenders out of the temple.

Clouds. Lots of sky and clouds. Clouds
of all sorts. Venus fixed on the left:
borne on the foaming crest of involution; Venus
on her wave: nothing, I repeat, nothing
but substance. February, twilight—wasn't it?—
lavender (green for youth, blue for love) sky—
a shadow, distinct, beautiful pink detail,

of all places on the pier with wood benches
near Canal Street . . .

The rain was like ice. The umbrella placed
over the phone booth. "I'm all right."
"What do you mean, what?" "Why don't you leave it
at that?" "Are you sure?" "Don't think that way."
"Yes, forever." And so on, the script proceeded.

AUGUST ABSTRACT

Then the presence of that absence,
a solid haze, dominating yellows

muted and mystic. Twenty-seventh Street
not too far from Eleventh Avenue,

a place (whose place?—but let it be clear
it must be someplace, this particular place,

and the place that the one who's abstracting
finds, a she or he finds, if it's been felt,

been felt between them, will have a name too)
in search of a form. The truth? The truth

that came to grieve, was aggrieved, for whom?
Truth determined alchemies of light.

Nearly dawn, half dark blue moon, half copper,
black stripes across it, above a round

neon clock next to the red and white
billboard in the shape of a toothpaste box,

the windblown river capped wave after wave.
Kokoschka's palette transposed . . . hot and still

with fact. That nothing was . . . nothing unbound. A sound, that sound, inside.

WHY NOT SAY WHAT HAPPENS?

I

Of icons. Of divination. Of Gods. Repetitions
without end. I have it in my notes,
a translation from the Latin, a commentary
on the Book of Revelation—"the greater
the concentration of power on earth,
the more truth is stripped of its power,
the holiest innocent, in eternity,
is 'as though slain . . .'"
It has nothing to do with the apocalyptic.
The seven-headed beast from the sea,
the two-horned beast from the earth, have always—
I know, I've studied it—been with us.
Me? I'm only an accessory to particular images.

II

According to the translation of the police transcript,
the sheikh—the arrested head
of the cell mockingly said—in a plot
involving a chemical attack,
needs, simply,
two or three young men with brains and training
with nothing to gain or lose,
not an army.
It doesn't take much these days to be a prophet.
Do you know how much poison can be put
in a ten-liter barrel?

You pour it and spread it, then you leave.
The web is, prosecutors believe,
so intricate, the detainee,
they think, may also be a member
of cells in Barcelona and Frankfurt.

III

Yet another latest version of another
ancient practice—mercenaries, as they were once known,
are thriving, only this time
they're called "private military contractors."
During the last few years their employees
have been sent to Bosnia, Nigeria, Colombia, and, of course,
most recently, Iraq. No one knows
how extensive the industry is, but some military experts
estimate a market of tens of billions of dollars.

IV

Autumn turned to winter and the site
began to clear. The limits of my language
are the limits of my world, said Wittgenstein.
The realization—the state of the physical world
depends on shifts in the delusional thinking
of very small groups. One of Garfinkle's patients
tripped over a severed foot while evacuating
the Stock Exchange. Several others saw

the first plane pass right next to the almost
floor-length windows of their conference room.
"When I'm not working, the last thing I want to do
is talk about it," said one policeman, who,
like many of the city's uniformed officers,
is still working a schedule of twelve hours on,
twelve hours off . . . Shoes, books, wallets, jewelry,
watches, some of them still keeping time . . .
The congressman says he can't say for sure
there isn't a suitcase with a nuclear bomb
floating around out there. Everything
immense and out of context. The large item
in the mud, one of the motors that powered
the Towers' elevators. "It's intense"—
says Lieutenant Bovine—"no photographs! This is
a crime scene!" What happened was one floor
fell on top of another, as many as ten floors
compressed into a foot of space. What fell
was mostly metal . . . The cement vaporized . . .
The Night Watch was what the laid-out scene
looked like. The fences around the wreckage
covered with T-shirts, teddy bears, and memorial
banners signed by thousands of visitors;
tourists snap pictures, and, subject to the way
the wind is blowing, the air is tinged
with an acrid smoke . . . "Lost/Missing Family
1-866-856-4167 or 1-212-741-4626 . . ." A Web Exclusive,
the poet will speak about poetry and grief . . .

The smells of burning wiring, dankness
from the tunnels, the sharp and sweet
cherrylike smell of death. At eight-ten on Friday
two more bodies are found in a stairwell
of the South Tower. Work, again, stops,
and the ironworkers, who have been cutting
steel beams, come out from the hole. The work
goes on until well past midnight. More debris
is removed, another body recovered. A group
of ironworkers stands on a gnarled beam,
one end of which juts over the pit
like a gangplank. Three 35-millimeter movie cameras
are placed on top of nearby buildings, each programmed
to take a picture every five minutes, day and night.
A bugler slips onto the site and plays "Taps."

V

That period of ten or eleven years—
concerning it I can express myself briefly.
At some point, in collective time, electronic space
turned into time. The miraculous
multiplication of loaves was restricted to the rentiers.
A grappa in a black, pyramid-shaped bottle
was taken cognizance of,
and, with no resistance,
for the most part, no guarantees
were made for the slow, the meek, or the poor of spirit,

who, for reasons unexplained,
allowed themselves to disappear
into the long, red evenings, night's early gray-blues.

VI

Screaming—those who could
sprinting—south toward
Battery Park, the dark cloud
funneling slowly—
there are two things you should know
about this cloud—
one, it isn't only ash and soot
but metal, glass, concrete, and flesh,
and, two, soon
any one of these pieces
of metal, glass, or concrete
might go through you.
As she turns to run, a woman's bag
comes off her shoulder,
bright silver compact discs sent
spinning along the ground, a man,
older, to the right,
is tripping,
falls against the pavement,
glasses flying
off his face.

VII

Have I mentioned my grandmother,
my father's mother, who died long ago
but who visits me in dreams?
It's to her, mostly, I owe
the feeling that, in cases of need,
those transfigured in eternal love help us
certainly with eternal,
and, perhaps, also, with temporal gifts;
that, in eternal love, all is gratis—
all that comes from eternal love
is gratis.

VIII

My father?—my father was a worker. I can still hear him
getting up in the morning to go to work.
Sadness, too, has to be learned,
and it took my father time to learn it,
but he did, though when he did
his tears were never chronic.
As for the economies on which my parents' lives depended,
they won't be found
in any book.

IX

It's the details that dream out
the plot. Rearrange the lies, the conceits,
the crimes, the exploitation
of needs and desires,
and it's still there, the whole system's
nervous system—inside it,
at times, a dreamer at work, right now
it's me. The air not yet too cold with winter,
at a sidewalk table at the Cornelia Street Cafe—
a dream, it's a dream, the dream
of a dream song, the dream of a dream,
a glass of Sancerre on the table, re-visioning,
in a purple mist, a tugboat, practical and hard,
as it approaches a freighter,
black, with the red-lettered name BYZANTIUM.

X

Capital? Careful! Capital capitalizes,
assimilates, makes
its own substance, revitalizing
its being, a vast metabolism absorbing even
the most ancient exchanges, running away,
as the cyberneticians put it,
performing, as it does, its own
anthropomorphosis, its triumph
the triumph of mediation—

and, let's not forget,
it organizes, capital organizes, capital is
"an organizing,"
organizing
social forms.

XI

Pink above the Hudson
against the shadows lingering still,
the sky above an even blue and changing
to a pale gray and rose.
A coat of snow in the park on Tenth Avenue,
clumps of grass sticking
out of it, late afternoon, in Druids,
Sam Cooke on the jukebox, lines
from an obscure tune from the box set,
"even my voice belongs to you,
I use my voice to sing, to sing, to sing to you . . ."
The lives of the two or three others who pass through
as close to you as the weather.
Walking back, the dotted lines
of the lights on the Bridge, the sun
blotted out by a burst of vermilion.

XII

I remember it—the gold burnt into gold,
the gold on gold and on white and yellow,
an incandescence condensing the sunlight,
outburning the sunlight, the factory
molten, the sun behind it, in it, thin,
gold, pig iron, a spray of fire, flywheels
revolving through the floor, rims almost
reaching the roof, enormous engines
throwing great pounding cylindrical arms
back and forth, as if the machines
are playing a game, trying to see how much
momentum can be withstood before one
or the other gives way. I remember—down Sixth
to Downing, to Varick, down Varick, downtown.
A cat is in the rubbish in the street. The sun
over Jersey. The gap at the end of West Street,
the sun on the clock tower. The melancholy
induced by the pressure of time, the wavering
ambitions, failed ideas, time wasted.
The unexpected breeze, warm, the sense
of the river. The sky blue, dark blue
yet pure in color, not blackened
or tarnished, above the low, old
buildings, like a painting of something
solid rather than the solid thing itself,
a high and low composition. But what
light there is in that landscape . . .

IN A MOOD

Less stupid than I seem, less
intelligent than I think. Observing

the subtlety innately a part of Near
Eastern manners, the mysterious

uses of power not entrusted to me.
Holy books' tribal signs inscribed

on skulls, a war—the Undersecretary
for Imperial Affairs says with a shrug—

is a lot more than a cosmic phenomenon.
In the spaciousness of syntax and text,

history's, or a history's, spaces composed,
the feeling, the meaning, aspired to,

the poem of an era. What will, indeed,
be revealed by the most expert lies

binds which economy, which comedy?
And all those memories in a mood.

Lilac-shaded shades of dark green
around the Bridge—that too, that evening.

A woman and a man beside the river . . .
A line consisting of a burning sky,

a sky on fire . . . the sky is on fire!
Then what, and then again what, unfolded . . .

UNYIELDINGLY PRESENT

Near the curb beside the police lines
a pool of blood, the gas tanks of the cars

in the garage on West Street
exploding, an air tank, its out-of-air

alarm going off, pops, and is skidding.
That woman staring into space, her dress

on fire. What transpires in
a second. On an intact floor

a globe of the world
bursts like a balloon. A ceiling-mounted

exit sign is melting. Facile equivalences
are to be avoided. Hell the horrific

into the routine. Glass and metal
can be identified, not the atoms

of human ash. I set down thoughts. Sequences
of images, of emotions, dissolved

in a mass, encoded in the brain.
The depth or the width of the hatred measured?

From so high up the time it takes for those
who are falling. Is it that reality, disjointed,

cannot be discerned, or that consciousness,
disjointed, cannot discern it?

The message I am communicating,
this beam of focused energy, no, I said,

no, I am not going to allow anything
to happen to you. I summon up

in my mind a place where my thoughts will find
yours—no, nothing is going to happen to you.

An issue of language now,
isn't it? There are these vicious circles

of accumulated causation.
Irreal is the word. I know of no

defense against those addicted to death. God.
My God. I thought it was over, absolutely

had to be. What am I supposed to feel?
Images that, after that, loop in the head.

Looming ahead, in the smoke, that man
at the railing can't breathe.

I'm having trouble breathing, he says.
You saw it? I saw it. I'm frightened.

This is about—which states of mind? Solid brown
and gray, a muddy mass of debris,

of powder. There is a strip of window glazing
hanging from—what kind of a tree?

What isn't separated, what isn't
scribbled, what will not be metamorphosed,

reduced, occurring, it will be said,
unyieldingly fixed, unyieldingly present . . .

NEWS BACK EVEN FURTHER THAN THAT

I

Dust, the dust of a dust storm;
yellow, black, brown, haze, smoke;
a baby photographed with half
a head; the stolen thoroughbred
a boy is riding bareback attacked
by a lion; the palace, fixed up
as a forward command post—"This,"
says Air-War Commander Mosely,
"would make a pretty nice casino";
why is such a detailed
description necessary?
that smell in the air is the smell
of burned human flesh;
those low-flying A-10 Warthogs
are, each of them, firing
one hundred bullets a second.

II

The President refuses to answer a question
he wasn't asked. The President denies
his eyes are the eyes of a lobster.
The map is being drawn: Mosul in the north,
Baghdad in the center, Basra in the south.
The news back even further than that:
"He Says He Is the Prophet Ezekiel.
In the Great Mudflats by the River Chebar,

He Has Seen, He Proclaims, Four Angels,
Each with Six Wings, on a Fiery Wheel."
Collaborators cut into pieces and burnt to death
in public, on spits, like lambs. In spray paint
across the armored personnel carrier:
"Crazy Train," "Rebel," "Got Oil? . . ." There,
on Sadoun Street, in a wheelbarrow, a coil
of wire, a carpet, rolled, Persian, antique.

III

"I've just been to see her. It's made her
mad—angry, yes, of course, but I mean mad,
truly mad. She spoke quietly, quickly—
maniacally. 'Wargame, they're using wargame
as a verb, they didn't wargame the chaos—
chaos! Do you think they care about
the chaos? The chaos just makes it easier for them
to get what they want. Wargame!
What they've wargamed is the oil,
their possession of the oil, what they've wargamed
is the killing, the destruction,
what they've wargamed is their greed . . .'
Had I noticed that Lebanon had become
an abstract noun, as in 'the Lebanonization of'?
'It may just as well have been two or three
atomic bombs, the amount of depleted
uranium in their bombs, the bombs

in this war, the bombs in the war before this—
uranium's in the groundwater now,
uranium is throughout the entire
ecology by now, how many generations
are going to be
contaminated by it, die of it, be poisoned by it? . . .'
War, a war time, without limits.
Technocapital war a part
of our bodies, of the body politic.
She quoted Pound—the *Pisan Cantos*—
she couldn't remember which—
there are no righteous wars.
'There is no righteous violence,'
she said, 'it's neurobiological
with people like this—
people who need to destroy and who need to kill
like this—and what we're seeing now
is nothing compared
to what we'll see in the future . . .' "

RUBAIYAT

The holes burned in the night.
Holes you can look through and see
the stump of a leg, a bloody
bandage, flies on the gauze; a pulled-up

satellite image of a major
military target, a 3-D journey
into a landscape of hills and valleys . . .
All of it from real-world data.

Zoom in close enough—the shadows
of statues, the swimming pools of palaces . . .
closer—a garden of palm trees,
oranges and lemons, chickens, sheep;

a map being sketched on a scrap
of paper; a fist coming down firmly
on the table; a tray with a dish
of lamb, and a bowl of rice and pine nuts.

Yes, that's it. I've become
too clear-sighted—the mechanics of power
are too transparent. Yes, that's
precisely it. The creation

of a deep-down pit, a slag heap
of broken masonry, of twisted metal,
a persistent ringing noise from inside—
as if thousands of telephones have been

left off the hook. Did you notice that?
The Pentagon's "Military Diaries
Project," soldiers starring in their own
war movies, training digital cameras

on themselves—a child is put
in a wheelbarrow after stepping on a mine.
Politics? Personified. His head
permanently cocked, he is attended

by a team of physicians
and an electronic-implant engineer.
He hopes he'll be able to confer
with the Shah of Iran in Cairo. "Dead?

The Shah? Really? No one's said a thing
to me about it," his response to the response
of a diplomatic press correspondent.
Poetry's not what's made impossible

by it—laughter is. Is it even
farce?—the translator, for example, who,
because of threats, is wearing a bulletproof
vest and a large pair of army goggles

for disguise, the sniper who slides
a condom over the muzzle of his gun
to keep the sand out. I try to get
the chronology straight . . . I look

out on the harbor, in the blue light.
I type into my machine. Perhaps
a glance at the newspaper. I listen
closely and I don't listen at all . . .

How complicated do you think the geopolitical
background behind all of this is? Brains
uprooted and warped, the logic's
schizophrenic. What's that again? A poem,

a speech, of lament, a threnody
A poem of thoughts, of consequences.
Time flows, is flowing, forward and back.
I lift a spoon, my hand is trembling. How many

corpses are counted and for what reasons?
That's what was said. The captured are blinded
except one blinded in one eye only
will lead the others back. What? War

as a living text? Cyberwar and permanent
war, Third Wave War, neocortical war,
Sixth Generation War, Fourth Epoch
War, pure war and war of computers

to process it, systems
to represent it, war of myth
and metaphor, of trope and assent,
war of hundreds of millions of televisions

assuring it, hundreds of billions
of dollars, a PK machine gun or two, a few
gunmen you can hire cheap, with their own
Kalashnikovs. Now . . . what now?

I want you to watch carefully
what I am saying now—are you
with me? An inch-long piece of steel,
part of the artillery shell's

casing, sliced through the right eye
into his brain, severely damaging
the optic nerve of his left eye,
spraying bone splinters

into the brain, making him quick to lose
his temper, so acutely sensitive to pain
the skin on his face hurts
when wind blows against it . . .

METAMORPHOSES (AFTER OVID)

I
Ineffable feeling and an elation
of the senses, sensibility

burning without bursting,
impossible to find a word or a gesture,

or a manner in which to express it, I go,
Apollo, God of sun and music,

of prophecy and healing, God of the poem, said,
I go wherever it takes me, he said, then stopped,

in a swoon. Venus's doing—
a revenge too complicated to get into:

he who sets the earth on fire
possessed by his love of Leucothoe.

Eyes only for her—each instant
intense; the violet in the morning light

is intense; the blue in the light around noon intense;
and, where the estuary curves,

this blinding light this late December afternoon
lasts as long as he thinks of her. No moon is eclipsed

between him and the earth:
it's he who's turning pale with love.

Her eyes are her mother's eyes—her mother's
and her mother's mother's eyes—the lightest,

the most blue, twilight eyes, twilight,
midnight, blue . . .

II
But, don't forget, there's evil.
Do you think a muse

will avoid evil? One's inspiration
polluted, one's imagination unhinged?

Every day she still sees him. Pyreneus,
the warlord, his militia in control

of the state. She was on Parnassus.
A shadow fell. The dark green air began

to quiver. Huge, widely spaced
drops, the heavens exploded.

Two of his thugs drove up, told her
to get in out of the rain. Took her

to his villa, into an inner room.
From his rococo chair upholstered

with silk, arms extended, he rose
to greet her. Designer jeans, white

T-shirt, yellow linen jacket, a warm,
silent gaze, his eyes

slightly protruding. His manner
obsequious and unctuous.

A bottle of whiskey on the table.
I understand, he said,

what power is. Understand—he has
deep sympathies, for children

especially. He must force himself
to execute any form of violence.

If only it would be recognized
it is his by right. He would have been

a connoisseur of painting, of music.
Instead obligations of destiny,

of divine order, of blood. Then
this—the sky cleared with an eerie

swiftness. Clouds thinned and parted,
a radiant sky, a fresh, electrical

fragrance in the air. She said
she wished to leave—he locked

the door . . . she climbed from the opened window
onto a breeze that carried

her away . . . Pyreneus,
then, as if in a seizure, raising himself

to his highest power, followed after her
into sky rushing down

around him in darkness, his skull
crushed on the bright green grass.

III

So she, Venus, entangled in the intricacies
of the time, having lost her composure,

immersed in fear, screaming to no effect
against the Fates' decrees of disaster,

the awful blackness behind the azure light,
the Furies' shadows behind the azure light,

her soul caught in the eyes of an owl seen
in one of a thousand streets, a grape seen

about to be eaten inside the mind, a phrase
snapped apart and fading away, a sentence

exclaimed to itself . . . a distant echo . . . in a state
of wounded wakefulness, in a wounded exhaustion . . .

wounded blood is being bought, wounded blood is sold,
bones are being unearthed, children's bones,

the light of Rome is a light that is bleeding,
destruction is in its fullest motion,

iconoclasts and iconolaters killing each other
before a Tomb of an Unknown Soldier.

IV

The final words of the book are being written—
have I made it?—light and sorrow and dream . . .

A discourse, any discourse—a particular
illustration of the species. The city,

all around, always there, ahead and behind.
The freighter, covered by the sun, nearing

the harbor. A slow, shapeless wheel is what
it feels like, the pressure deep and silent.

The ferry will be arriving, a yellow and black dot—
someone will be waiting. The book of a man,

the book of a woman, the book of the city . . .
the partial, vertical episodes that come out of nowhere . . .

Power knows of no argument other than power, he said,
power makes of its own power as much as it can.

Ugliness, when truly touched, the shock of beauty
is what turns the game around. Poetry,

what a game, sad, sad-eyed Paul Celan said,
poetry, language that is particularly fated.

The harbor. An island. A flock of gulls. The sea.
Those clouds are being driven inland from the sea.

The gray and purple sky . . . unfathomable.
So on we went. If she had not said it,

the journey would not have been taken.
Sometimes I felt a little dizzy, even

structurally unstable. The world once more
the means by which the meek are to be

brought to their knees. Not the poet
espousing simplicities, shifting the props. To whom

can one make this clear? A poetry of autonomies,
bound by a transcendent necessity. Plato's idea

of anamnesis, what is in us is remembered,
that which we are destined, in thoughts and in images,

to give expression to. Concentration
aural and visual. A table covered with pages of notes

I compose as I feel. Through my beginning
through to my end, my moira, my allotted part.

When this time comes to its end, what I don't write
will not exist. I did my work, lived

as if the day, my own day, had come. I was, I am,
who I will be. I will not be eternally condemned.

WHAT IS THERE TO UNDERSTAND?

The competition between associations,
the final, ultimate, self. Him? Her?
He, she, are transfigured. Nothing
has changed, only they have.

                              Understand?
That pain has receded into the darkness
it came from. The angel in the mind—
in a sudden hot place, in the focus of heat and excitement.

The Poem of the Intimate Core of an Abstract Feeling,
The Poem of Everything Is a Dream,
The Poem of Yes, There Is Something Personal Behind All This,
The Poem of the Slaughterers Who Believe in What They Say,
   Too,
are a prayer heard in motets.

A YEAR AGO THIS JUNE

There really was no avoiding the fact.
The suicide car bombing killing twelve,
wounding thirteen—when?
A year ago this June? "It can't go on like this,
you know, you'll see, take it from me,
something will happen—each false thing
must come to its end," he said,
then exploded in such forceful laughter
I couldn't tell if he was serious or joking . . .

I'll let you in on a secret. One's deepest secret
is a certainty that protects against the world.
Having wept and having thought,
suddenly, they're gone—what does it mean,
they're gone? The sun covered—
a gold expanse . . . the single star
over the harbor . . .

                    But that's another story.
The sulfuric acid was real, as were the small,
dry burrs stuck to the God's hair.
Who can measure
what determines the portion of an era
allotted to—but what can you do?
Black crosses are
tattooed on the prisoners' backs—black crosses!
Twelve hours of video digital discs already recorded.

IN THE SHAPE OF FATE OVER MY FATHER'S BIRTH

The circling of stars and wind, a clear,
cold, April night, his mother is climbing
the stairs, the grapevine beside the fence
by the alley, a shape of a fate with dark eyes
and a smile, a door opening, my grandfather
placing a hat on the couch in the sunroom,
he, my father, dressed in white in the oval
of the portrait, formally posed, the candle
in his left hand the Easter candle blessed
on Palm Sunday.

My mother was so afraid, her fingers so tightly
clamped my father couldn't separate them.
She couldn't move her body—now he can't move his.
When she couldn't speak words anymore, she spoke
in sounds, eyes widening and changed in color,
her head tilted sideways—now he can't
speak words, his head tilted sideways.

Silence. Sleepless. A fever. The Trumbell streetcar screeched
on the switch. The rattling, old, yellow Owl Cars late at night
into the morning—he likes
what he hears, a frying pan struck with the sizzle of butter,
the boning knife sliced through the leg of lamb
through to the cutting board . . .

Silence. The silence. The elm buds against the snow—
green spring snow. The spring equinox—his birthday. Sunday—

Sunday-silent snow.
Crossing Jefferson—in the park near the Whittier Hotel.
"It's a painting"—she pointed to the poplars in a line
to the river—"a painting," she said, the green,
the gray, river . . .

What? What? What is it? No, it isn't pain . . .
His voice. He can still hear his voice.

THE SINGLE NECESSITY

Those days eternities went through everything.
The extraneous—
that which is not experienced and imagined
in detail.
I observed a loose strand of her hair on her forehead
and loved her even more.

HISTORY FOR ANOTHER TIME

It was, of course,
impossible to have predicted the economic
cycle had peaked, perhaps the most . . .
what's the word? remarkable?—
perhaps the most remarkable period
in the history of capitalism. A little over
a three-hundred-seventeen-point drop in the Dow
in one day, only a few points' recovery the day after that.
Here was an item—forty-five-ish,
tall, with wire-frame glasses,
curly gray hair, his background
is in cable. He says
he has his visions. HorizontalNet
establishes separate Web sites
or horizontal portals—hortals he calls them—
for the waste management industry. Incidentally,
he wonders, do I have any idea how easy it is
to convert a digital watch into a timer?—
that all you've got to do is use
lightbulb filaments to ignite cotton
soaked in nitrocellulose, and you've got yourself
a detonated bomb.

                Look, it's on the record.
When asked to explain a personal motive
he may have had for the war, the President
unzipped his fly, took out his quite sizable member,
and replied, "Motive? You want my personal motive?

My personal motive is right here."
A massacre of eight hundred thousand
during the last hundred days is reported.
A rumor the rat is the newest unit of currency.
A skull, a child's shoe, stick out of the rubble in a room
on the church grounds where the dead
number over ten thousand. Rain-soaked mattresses,
lampshades, rotting piles of clothing
in heaps inside artillery-shelled houses.
Rats, I think I said, are being considered
as the unit of currency by the new government.

Pressure is what
it's about, and pressure's incalculable—
which eludes the historian. For a charge
of ten percent above the official rates,
weapons of every caliber can be supplied
from any country, be it North or South American,
Asian, or European. The whole world sells arms
through this consortium. Implements for killing
are among the most lucrative of commodities.
Supposedly, he and his son, and his son's
associates, have a sort of de facto monopoly
on the banana trade with Iran, linking his family
with the present occupants of the Baabda Palace.
That disturbance had no clear perimeter.
While some streets appeared safer than others,
there really was nowhere to hide. By midday

bands of looters were moving in waves
toward the small strip of shopping centers.
At one point men and women on the street
screamed, a red, seventies-vintage Cadillac
careened down the boulevard, its occupants
sitting on the edges of opened car windows
brandishing axes, the sky still bright at this end
of the city, the smoke and the sirens miles away,
at least for the time being. It is—it always is—
beginning again. It's unreal, the extent to which
all political discourse is the same. Legal relations
arising out of economic relations—Engels, isn't it?
I can't remember where I read it. Let me see
if I can remember. These days it's child's play
to figure out how things worked, as Brecht did—
in phase one, competitive capital,
or phase two, imperialism—to find the metaphors
to express it. Each phase had its machines
(in phase one, steam-driven motors, electric
or combustion motors in phase two) and its critical
structure (realism in the first phase, modernism
in the second). The present phase,
with its electronic and its nuclear-powered motors—
the era of after, or postmodernism—has proven
more difficult to configure. Its characteristic
machine, the computer, contains no emblematic
power. You can no more describe the heart
of a computer than the heart of a multinational

corporation. What's at the heart of a global
network of microcircuits? What is ancient
isn't what is chronologically the oldest
but that which emerges from the innermost
laws of time. Imagining how the universe
made its "quantum leap from eternity into time."
The universe bringing itself into being
by the accumulation of trillions upon trillions
of quantum interactions, the universe,
microscopically, forced by itself into being,
the consequence of which is that the past has no existence
except in the present. If the creation
of the universe happens outside time,
it must happen all the time, the big bang
here and now, the foundation of every instant . . .
The sudden breaking and tearing of space . . .
That ancient story, how they, in the combining
of their forms, in the necessity and logic
of purest form, in the logic of a dream—
the dimensions are inverted, and that place,
immense, is small now, the two of them
a dot on the red horizon. Neither seriousness
nor laughter is much help, either. You need only
be approached by one of the beggars
in Pennsylvania Station to see that certain rules
prevail in our midst. Still I,
for one, don't condone cut-off ears . . .

THAT TOO

A long walk up West Street along the piers.
The sky—right now the sun,
the clouds, a few seconds of light yellow.

The deepest being being a longing
to satisfy the longing for a solitude of two.

Gertrude Stein's "Composition as Explanation," that too.

Surely the blacks and golds
are the depth of a late October afternoon. Surely
the blues and greens fired by crimson are the sea.

THE GAME CHANGED

The phantasmic imperium is set in a chronic
state of hypnotic fixity. I have absolutely
no idea what the fuck you're talking about
was his reply, and he wasn't laughing,
either, one of the most repellent human beings
I've ever known, his presence a gross and slippery
lie, a piece of chemically pure evil. A lawyer—
although the type's not exclusive to lawyers.
A lot of different minds touch, and have touched,
the blood money in the dummy account
in an offshore bank, washed clean, free to be
transferred into a hedge fund or a foreign
brokerage account, at least half a trillion
ending up in the United States, with more to come.
I believe I told you I'm a lawyer. Which has had
little or no effect on a certain respect
I have for occurrences that suggest laws
of necessity. I too am thinking of it
as a journey—the journey with conversations
otherwise known as the *Divina Commedia*
is how Osip Mandelstam characterized Dante's poem.
Lebanon? I hear the Maronite Patriarch
dares the Syrians to kill him, no word
from my grandfather's side of the family
in the Shouf. "There are circles here"—
to quote the professor of international
relations and anthropology—"Vietnam, Lebanon,
and Iraq . . . Hanoi, Beirut, and Baghdad."

The beggar in Rome is the beggar in Istanbul,
the blind beggar is playing saxophone,
his legs covered with a zebra-striped blanket,
the woman beside him holding an aluminum cup,
beside them, out of a shopping bag, the eyes
of a small, sick dog. I'm no pseudoaesthete.
It's a physical thing. An enthusiasm,
a transport. The melancholy is ancient.
The intent is to make a large, serious
portrait of my time. The sun on the market
near Bowling Green, something red, something
purple, bunches of roses and lilacs. A local
issue for those of us in the neighborhood.
Not to know what it is you're breathing
in a week when Black Hawk helicopters resume
patrolling the harbor. Two young men
blow themselves up attaching explosives
on the back of a cat. An insurgency:
commandos are employed, capital is manipulated
to secure the oil of the Asian Republics.
I was walking in the Forties when I saw it—
a billboard with a background of brilliant
blue sky, with writing on it in soft-edged,
irregularly spaced, airy-white letters
already drifting off into the air, as if they'd
been sky-written—"The World Really Does
Revolve Around You." The taxi driver rushes
to reach his family before the camp is closed—

"There is no way I will leave, there is no way—
they will have to kill us, and, even if
they kill every one of us, we won't leave." Sweat
dripping from her brow, she picks up the shattered,
charred bones. She works for the Commission
on Missing Persons. "First they kill them,"
she says, "then they burn them, then they cover them
with dead babies . . ." Neither impenetrable opacity
nor absolute transparency. I know what I'm after.
The entire poem is finished in my head. No,
I mean the entire poem. The color, the graphic
parts, the placement of solid bodies in space,
gradations of light and dark, the arrangements
of pictorial elements on a single plane
without a loss of depth . . . This habit of wishing—
as if one's mother and father lay in one's heart,
and wished as they had always wished—that voice,
one of the great voices, worth listening to.
A continuity in which everything is transition.
To repeat it because it's worth repeating. Immanence—
an immanence and a happiness. Yes, exquisite—
an exquisite dream. The mind on fire
possessed by what is desired—the game changed.

ONCE AGAIN

The esplanade. High summer.
The sea is beyond

the sunset's light—
the shapes amassed, the sky

a current carrying us along,
heavy with that green and that black.

Fate's precisive wheel revolving,
force's writhing wheel—

the stealing, the killing, accomplished
by new types of half-monsters—

it's what I said—
the poem is the dream, a dream technique;

the primary soul-substance
on which our attention is fixed—

supernal, metaphysical—in other words,
a representation,

as we have seen,
of mythical origins.

Something felt, something needed—
as much as we needed;

a woman, a man,
love's characters, the myth

their own. We are agreed.
The moon is low, its silent flame

across the garden of roses, almost level
with the harbor. We place our hands

on the silence
and, once again, repeat the vow.

(LV) **DATE DUE** J

SEP 11 2006

WITHDRAWN

GAYLORD   PRINTED IN U.S.A.